ADAM JENSON

ARTIFICIAL INTELLIGENCE

A MODERN APPROACH

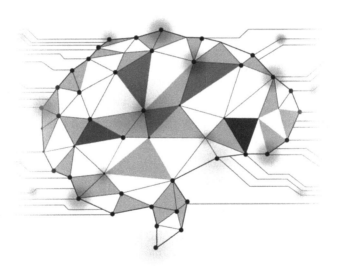

THE FUTURE IS COMING!

DISCOVER HOW ARTIFICIAL INTELLIGENCE WILL
CHANGE YOUR LIFE!

Table of Contents

Introduction

The following chapters will discuss everything you need to know about artificial intelligence and how you are using it in your day-to-day life. So much comes with artificial intelligence, and learning how to put this to work and how we are already using it is one of the best ways to see how this kind of technology can benefit us now and in the future. This guidebook took over many different topics about artificial intelligence so we can see how it is meant to work for us.

In the beginning of this guidebook, we are going to explore more what artificial intelligence is all about. We will look at how this process works, why it is so important, and other information on how this kind of technology works and how we may already be using this technology in our day to day life, without even noticing it.

The second part of this guidebook will

tackle how artificial intelligence is already being used in many different industries in so many ways. Almost any industry can benefit from using it, but these companies are leading the pack and are working on using this technology already. We will explore what artificial intelligence can do in various industries such as financial institution, marketing, medical field, and more.

In the next part of this guidebook, we will explore a bit of the different parts of artificial intelligence and some of the concerns that people may have when it comes to this kind of technology. We will be looking at whether or not society has been able to accept AI now and in the future and if it will replace our jobs. Also, we will be tackling some of the benefits, disadvantages, and ethical considerations of AI and using the technologies that come with it.

To end this guidebook, a few more topics will be discussed that will help us be more successful such as machine learning and how this works with artificial intelligence and how this can do some amazing things all on its own. And then we end with a fun discussion about the future of artificial intelligence and how this kind of technology will be able to shape our world and our future.

There are so many topics to discuss when it comes to artificial intelligence! And when we look at all of the different ways it affects our world already today, especially since it is so new, it is exciting to think of where this is going to head in the future. When you are ready to learn more about artificial intelligence and how it works in our modern lives, make sure to check out this guidebook to help you get started.

There are plenty of books on this subject on the market, so thanks again for choosing this one! Every effort was made to ensure it is full of as much useful information as possible, please enjoy!

Chapter 1

What is Artificial Intelligence?

The world of technology is rapidly changing, and being able to keep up with it all is sometimes a big challenge that businesses, and even individuals, struggle with. This makes it hard to know what will come next, and even whether or not using some of the technology is in the best interest of the business. Many times, we watch to see how the rest of the business world takes on a topic and hope to learn how it works and whether or not it is the right option for us.

Artificial intelligence is one of the technologies that is starting to take over the world. When most people hear about this, they go on a journey through sci-fi, thinking about how a computer could learn to take over the world. While it is true that some parts of artificial intelligence can train the computers you are using and can help them do some processes as a human can, this AI cannot match up to its applications and take over the world at all.

With this kind of idea in mind, we must take some time to learn more about artificial intelligence and how it is supposed to work, as well as how we can use it to help with our business, no matter which industry we are in. Many parts have to come together when we talk about artificial intelligence, so we must have a good understanding of some of the basics and how this all comes together and works.

Let us dive right in. AI, or artificial intelligence, is a subset of computer science that is set up to emphasize the creation of machines and systems seen as intelligent and that will be able to react and work in a manner that is similar to what we see with humans. There are many activities that a machine can do using AI which is designed to help with including speech recognition, problem-solving, learning, and planning to name a few.

To keep things simple, when we work with artificial intelligence, we work with the computer science. However, computer science is very large; artificial intelligence is just a part of it. In particular, AI is the process that can help us create machines and systems containing intelligence and can act and think on their own. And because of the power we see with these systems, it becomes a very essential part of our technology industry, and more businesses and companies start adding this in as well.

Research that we have been able to perform on AI has become specialized and highly technical. This is due to a few different factors including the nature of how artificial intelligence works and all of the various parts that come with it. Some of the core components that we can do with artificial intelligence were listed before, and as a business, you can probably go through and figure out how you can use the technology for each one by the time we get to the end of this guidebook.

Remember that knowledge is power when we work on artificial intelligence, and this knowledge engineering is so important to the core research we see with this field. Machines are trained to learn how to react and act in a way that is similar to humans, but only after the programmer has been able to provide them with enough information about how the world works and how the machine needs to behave in different situations.

We have to realize here that the machine or computer that uses AI does not just sit around and gain knowledge without any help. The computer has some limitations based on the information and examples that you decide to give to it, and the learning that it can do during that time can end up wrong if you do not train the system in the right way or if it was given wrong examples. The machine requires the programmer to give accurate information before it can behave in the manner that you would like.

To make sure that you can get the artificial intelligence to work properly, you have to provide it with access to things like objects, properties, categories, and relations between all the parts to implement the idea of the knowledge you want it to have. This will show us why this kind of process is not something that all businesses want to spend their time on. Being able to take the time to teach a computer how to behave like a human and how to work with topics like common sense, problem-solving, and reasoning is difficult and can take up a lot of time. While this amazing technology and all of the things that it can do can astound a lot of people, it may not always make sense in the time and cost commitments you have to handle.

As we go through this, we need to try and keep the whole process of artificial intelligence as simple and easy to understand as possible. AI comes onto the scene and makes it easier for a machine to learn from the past experiences that they have had; the machine can also learn how to adjust to any input that the user sends to it, much like a human can do. Most of the examples that are already present in the world when it comes to AI rely on a combination of deep learning and natural language processing. And when we use these kinds of technologies on a day-to-day basis, the computer will go through some training to finish the task that we want, simply by being trained on the right algorithm that will help it to see patterns, process lots of data, and more.

The next part of the equation that we want to spend some time here is the importance of artificial intelligence in many different fields--what this process is all about and how to use it for your own business. AI is starting to take over the world, and the process of learning how to use it for your business needs can help your performance and help you to beat out the competition.

AI automates some of the repetitive learning that goes on in a company, and it is more set up to handle the search for discoveries as it goes through the data. It is a bit different than what companies may be used with the hardware-driven robotic automation. Instead of going through and turning the manual tasks on automatically, AI works on frequent, computerized, and high volume tasks reliably and without wearing out in the process. To make sure that this kind of automation is up and running, a human inquiry has to happen as well so that the system knows what it is doing and how to behave along the way.

To add to this, AI makes sure that the product you already have will come with enough intelligence to do the job. In many cases, AI is not sold with the help of an individual application. Instead, the products you have chosen to use to run your business are going to be improved with the help of AI being added to them. Many machines that are considered "smart" are set up to combine with all of the data the company can hold onto to make sure that no matter what kind of field we are in, the technology can see improvements.

AI can also help us out when it comes to some of the progressive learning algorithms out there so that the data is in charge of the programming. AI can find any of the structures or the similarities that show up in the data to help the algorithm to gain a new skill. This algorithm turns into either a classifier or a predictor based on what you are trying to do with the algorithm. So, just like we will see with a bit of machine learning and how the algorithm can teach itself the right steps to doing some action, such as playing chess, it can use this idea to do a recommendation system or something else that you would like it to accomplish.

From here, we need to get the models to adapt when they receive some new data into the mix. Back propagation is a popular technique that AI can use to make sure that the chosen model can do the work it should and make adjustments, through the new data added and through the training, if you find that the answer it gives in the beginning is not the right one for you.

AI works then on analyzing the deep data and more of it with the use of neural networks that comes with many hidden layers. For example, when you work with a system that can detect fraud, which is something a lot of financial institutions and banks try and do, artificial intelligence can help with that, even though this kind of system was pretty much unheard of just a few years ago.

The next thing is the accuracy of the artificial intelligence when it comes to the work it does, thanks to the neural networks and other algorithms that come with it. For example, when you interact with voice recognition software like Alexa, you know that it can learn your voice and your requests, and it will become good at making predictions and knowing what you would like it to accomplish after just using it for a short amount of time.

Compared to a lot of the other methods of technology that have tried to do this in the past, AI is the best method to use because it knows how to read this information and sort through it. AI is the method that can learn on its own by sorting through all of that data and ensuring that you get the answers you are looking for in the process. Other techniques have attempted to do this in the past, but nothing has worked like AI has done.

Due to the currently available algorithms and how they handle the learning process differently than a human can, we must see how they work and how the algorithms attempt to take in the world around them. This can be beneficial because it ensures that things get done quickly and that the machine or system you are using can catch on to the relationships and patterns found in a large amount of data, often ones that humans lose track of or cannot find themselves. This human to AI partnership, meaning that even with all of the neat things that AI can do, having a human around to work with the algorithm and look over important data, offers us with a lot of different opportunities and benefits as follows:

1   It can help us to bring in some more analytics to industries and domains that previously were not using this technology to its full potential.

2   This relationship can also come into play to improve the performance in existing analytic technologies. This includes things like series analysis and computer vision to name a few options.

3   It can be used to help break down some of the present barriers of economics. This could also include language and translation barriers.

4   It is there to augment some of the abilities that are already out there and helps us to improve on the jobs that we are already doing right now.

5   This new relationship provides us with a much better vision than before, along with more understanding, a better memory than what we can do on our own, and more time, all with the help of some artificial intelligence mixed in.

Even though there are a lot of benefits to utilizing all that artificial intelligence can provide to us, some challenges come with it as well. Artificial intelligence can change up every industry when it is used correctly. So many industries have already started to use what is available with AI, and more and more industries likely use these as well to help them get better at their work.

With this in mind, it is important for every industry and company that is interested in artificial intelligence to understand that this system can have some limits. One of the principle limitations that will show up with the use of AI is that it learns from the data. There is no other way in which we can incorporate the knowledge and the data we want the system to have.

This means if the data has parts that are not filled in, or inaccurate parts, it will then be reflected in the outcome. And any additional layers of analysis and prediction have to be added into this separately.

Artificial intelligence is not just about one or two things; it is a whole umbrella of terms and technologies and techniques that are all meant to come together to change the way we teach computers how to behave and how to make something learn. Some of the different parts that come together when we are looking at artificial intelligence include:

Machine learning

This is a subset of artificial intelligence and can work to automate the building process of analytical models. It uses a lot of different methods to make these models including physics, operations research, statistics, and neural networks. These are all also used to find any insights that are hidden in the data without it having to be programmed to know where to look or what predictions to make in the process.

A neural network

This is a type of machine learning that has many different interconnected units, similar to what we find in the brain and with neurons, which will process the information by responding to given inputs. This information is then relayed between each of the units. The process requires us to have many passes at the data to make sure that we can find the connections and that the system then derives some kind of meaning and predictions from the undefined data.

Deep learning

This uses a huge level of neural networks, which come with many layers of processing units, and this allows it to take advantage of advances in computer power and improved training techniques. This is all done for the machine to learn some of the more complex patterns found in a big amount of data. Speech and image recognition are two of the applications that use this.

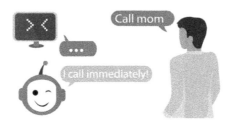

Cognitive computing

This is another subfield of AI that helps us to get a natural interaction to occur with the machines. Using AI with this cognitive computing comes with the goal for the machine to naturally simulate the processes of humans through the ability to interpret speech and images.

Computer vision

This relies on pattern recognition, along with some deep learning, to recognize what is showing up in a video or a picture. When the machines can process, analyze, and then understand the image it sees, they have a much better chance at capturing videos and images in real-time, and then they can interpret what goes on in its surroundings.

AI is already coming into the mix and causing a lot of different industries to change up the way that they do things. It is there to ensure that we can do our jobs more efficiently and effectively, to speed up a lot of processes to a speed that a lot of humans will never be able to accomplish, as well as to make life easier for customers and the business all at the same time. When you are ready to learn more about which industries benefits from AI the most and how this technology is already in use, and how it can be brought in even more in the future, then take some time to read the following chapters and see just how amazing AI can be.

Chapter 2

How AI Has Been Able to Change the World of Finance

The first area we are going to explore when it comes to AI and what it can do for you and other businesses is in the world of finance. A lot of different financial institutions like to take a look at the capabilities of AI because it helps them to do their job more efficiently. This may sound silly, but it works at helping to assess the amount of risk that a bank or another financial company would take when they take on a new customer; it even helps the system to detect fraud.

When we take a look at all of the hundreds of thousands and more transactions that a bank and other financial companies have to deal with constantly, no wonder that using AI make things popular. There is no way that a human would be able to go through all of that information and detect fraud all of the time, for example. But fraud, when it is not caught, can cost the bank a ton of money in the process. With the help of AI, a lot of money can be saved, allowing the bank to serve their customers a whole lot better.

Now, a few different methods can be used to help the financial world with the use of AI. Some of these may not even be methods that you thought out right off the bat, but they all help the banking industry to become better at the job they do and ensures that you will get better customer service in the process as well. Some of the top ways that AI has been able to break into the financial world and make things better and more efficient includes:

Assessing the Amount of Risk

Since AI can take in large amounts of data and then learn from these, it is natural that it would do well with all of the data that a financial institution can feed to it, even in the training models, much less on a day-to-day basis. Most financial institutions have hundreds of thousands of transactions in a week, which can help the AI algorithm learn how to behave and what it can do in no time at all. And this makes it better at its job, faster, more efficient, and can provide more safety and security for your finances.

Let us take a look just at how credits cards are used, managed, and even given out. Today, you are expected to use a credit score just to figure out whether or not you can be eligible for one of these cards. However, being able to group people into those who are have nots and haves is not always the most efficient method to use for a business. Instead, data about the individual that could include how many credit cards they have, their current active loans, their payment habits, and more can be used in order to personalize the eligibility of the individual and to customize the amount of interest rate allowed on the card that makes the most sense to the financial institute.

While this can help the consumer and the financial institution, we have to look at what kind of system would be able to put this together and make it all happen. And the simple answer is AI. Since this is all about data, being dependent and driven by data, scanning through all of the records that the financial institution has been able to get on their customers can give the AI tool the ability to make smarter and fast recommendations on credit offerings and loans. And they are more efficient and accurate at doing this than a professional loan officer as well.

Machine learning and AI start taking the place of a human analyst quickly as inaccuracies in this kind of field can cost millions. Ai is based on machine learning, which means that the program learns how to do the job better over time. This allows for a lower possibility of mistakes in the process. So, while it may take some time to get this program to work the way that we want and to get it all set up and ready to go, the more that the program is used in this kind of matter, the better it will get.

As you can see, this process and the use of AI help not just the business but also the customer in many different ways. The business will of course benefit — otherwise they would not waste their time using AI at all — because they can get through the loan application at a much faster rate and make sure that the individuals who need the money get it quickly. They can earn the interest payments in the process as well once the loan goes out and gets started too. While we may be seeing some inaccuracies show up with the algorithms used, these are much fewer and less costly than what we see with a human loan officer.

Detecting and Managing Fraudulent Charges

Fraud is a big issue for any financial institution. It causes them to lose out on a lot of money along the way as they have to go back and reimburse the person who had their money taken wrongly, and then they have to catch the person who did it. These charges can cost the financial institution a lot of money in the long term, and this gets expensive and hard to work with. No customer wants to work with a bank that cannot protect their money and their assets either.

With all of the many transactions that we can see going through a financial institution on a day-to-day basis, and with all of the different types of loans, people, and more filtering their way through there, banks have a lot on their plate, and they want to make sure that they can watch out for any transactions that try to sneak in that are not supposed to be there. If these charges get through and are not monitored and stopped at the right time, it can end up costing the bank or financial institution a lot of money in the process and a loss of reputation in many cases.

All financial institutions and many other businesses need to be able to find the best methods to use to reduce the amount of present risk. This is very much true when we are looking at the savings and checking and even the credit card usage of an individual customer. If you are given a loan, whether it is to fix up your home or for a car or something else, you are being handed the money that someone else has in their account. This is why banks have to be careful about how much they hand out and at what terms along the way. This is also why if you have an account of some kind, you are going to earn a bit of interest in the process as well.

To make sure that the bank can keep lending out money and earning interest, and that they do not scare their customers away, they have to make sure that they are providing good customer service and keeping some of the fraudulent charges out of the place. This is sometimes harder to do than it seems, and sometimes, they do not do a good job in terms of what we hear with data breaches and more. But AI can make this detection much easier and more effective in the process.

This is also another reason why these financial institutions are very serious about fraud. AI is on top when it comes to helping these companies to identify fraud and any security issues. It can take a look at all of the spending behaviors that are normal and allowed in the past, and even through different instruments, to figure out when some behavior seems a bit odd and needs to be checked out and even stopped. For example, if a credit card is from someone in Nebraska and was used there at 10 AM, and then at 11 AM, a transaction went through in Germany, some form of fraud is likely going on, and the AI tool can spot this.

Or maybe, the AI algorithm is looking at an account, and it has a pretty good idea of how the user takes out money, how much, when, and so on. Then, there comes a time when someone else tries to withdraw a sum of money that seems unusual for that kind of account or withdrawal after that person was already there for the day. These are things that the AI system in this industry can help out with.

Offering New Products to Customers

How many times have you been offered a new product from your bank or financial institution? It could be a new banking account, a new way for you to get onto your account, or another product that can help you to get the results that you would like out of your account. All of these were done thanks to machine learning and the algorithms the bank was able to create to sort through data.

Basically, your financial institution spent some time gathering up data on what customers were looking for the most when it came to their chosen bank. They would look through surveys, what others in the industry are doing, and even social media to figure this out. This hopefully was a large amount of data, but it can be overwhelming to work with and the bank or financial institution has to take it a bit further and bring in machine learning.

Through the process of organizing and

cleaning the data, and working with data preprocessing, they were able to get the data ready to go through the necessary algorithms to learn what insights and hidden patterns are found in that large source of data. Machine learning is the driving force that comes with these algorithms and will ensure that you have the right information that you need to handle the data, and get it ready to read through.

There are a number of algorithms to use, and the type of data the bank decided to use is going to be a big determining factor in the algorithm that they choose to work with. But in the end, the goal is to help them learn more about their customers and what products and services they should offer to their customers. And this is why certain products and services and incentives are offered through your bank at different times.

Saves the Financial Institution Money

When we are able to work through the different parts that we have discussed in this chapter, we can find that it saves a financial institution, and potentially you as their customer, a lot of money. When the financial institution is able to learn what products sell the best, and can keep the number of fraudulent charges down to a minimum, it can save them a lot of money, and can help them to do their job more efficiently.

Take the fraudulent charges. These can potentially cost the financial institution millions of dollars a year. It is hard to keep financial information hidden and secure in the manner that we should, and this leads to a lot of problems with information getting stolen, and money not being used by the account holder. As someone who holds the account, you do not want to be liable for charges that you did not personally do or approve. But the bank also doesn't want to swallow those charges, get stuck with them, or spend all of that time investigating and trying to get the money back.

With artificial intelligence and machine learning, it is possible to catch the fraudulent charges ahead of time, and saves these financial institutions millions of dollars a year. Keeping up with all of the transactions that happen among all of the customers is impossible to do manually by anyone, and is just asking for a lot of these charges to get missed. But artificial intelligence is able to keep up with it all, watch for a number of factors that will show up in fraudulent charges, and then alerts the right people, perhaps even putting a hold on the account until someone can come look at it. This ensures that the customers information and finances remain secure, and can save the bank a lot of money.

This is also true when the financial institution is trying to determine whom to loan out money to. There are always a lot of individuals who will apply for a loan, a credit card, or a mortgage through these banks, but not all of them are likely to pay the money back. Sometimes they just have a bad payment history in the past and they are too risky to take back on. Other times the amount of money they are asking for is too much.

With the artificial intelligence, the bank can know ahead of time who is the most likely to pay back the money, and who they may need to decline, or charge a higher amount of interest to in order to save themselves. Having customers default on a loan is never a good thing for the bottom line of a bank, and it is going to cause them, and other customers, a lot of lost money in the process. With artificial intelligence, the bank can tell ahead of time who is the best candidate for them to loan money to, and who they are likely to get that money back from, and this helps them when determining who they should lend money out to in the first place.

Sure, it is possible that a loan officer would be able to do this on their own, but humans make errors, and may miss out on some things as well. Plus, often these systems are put in place to review the loan application, and then pass on the ones that are promising to a loan officer, who gets the final say. This saves a lot of time and hassle for the loan officers, who may be overworked already, and can speed up the amount of time it takes to hear back about an application.

With the help of artificial intelligence, the bank or financial institution is able to explore the best customers to offer loans to, and ensures that they will get the full amount back plus the agreed upon interest. Rather than losing out on a customer who doesn't pay back the money, and having to swallow the costs of that, artificial intelligence ensures that the financial institution is saving money and only loaning out money to those who are good risks.

These are just a few of the methods that can come into play when helping a financial institution save money. These companies need to make sure that they are able to offer the best services to their customers, protect the money that their customers have in their accounts, and so much more. And when they are able to add in some of the benefits and features that come with artificial intelligence, it is not only easier to make sure that all of the above tasks happen and are taken care of, but also help this company to save a lot of money; savings that they can then pass on to their customers in higher interest rates, better loan terms, and so much more in the process.

These are just a few of the methods that show us how AI can come into play when we look at the financial world. Many people may not think that the financial world, or many other industries, are going to benefit when it comes to working with AI, but as we can see in this chapter, the financial world can protect their customers and really become more efficient at their work with the help of AI and some of the other technologies that come with it.

Chapter 3

How AI Has Changed How the Medical Field Function

Another area where AI can change the world is in the medical field. It is working to improve and make work more efficient in the medical field in a lot of different ways, and as more advances in this kind of technology become more common, it is likely to that we will see it even more than before. This is good news for those who are looking to get into the medical field or those who want to ensure that their quality of life keeps going up in the process as well.

There are a lot of ways that AI can help out with various parts of the medical world, even if we may not realize it right now. Being on the outside, looking in, it may seem like we are not seeing much of this. But often, a lot of the procedures and results you get from the doctor will be given thanks to some of the AI technology. With this in mind, let us take a look at some of the ways that AI has already made an influence on the medical field!

Analyzing Images

Right now, many of the providers you visit see many different images at a time. The provider has to stop throughout their day and look at images of the brain, X-rays of all kinds, ultrasounds, and so much more to help them see what is wrong with their patient. And each patient may need this kind of imaging done, though it is not as likely that everyone will need this. But if the doctor has 50 patients, and half of them need some kind of imaging done during that visit, then the doctor has a lot of information to look over and make a diagnosis from.

But, maybe, it does not need to be this way. It is possible that with the help of AI, the provider would be able to work with a machine to help look over the images and come out with a good diagnosis in just a few minutes, and sometimes faster, rather than the provider having to do all of the work themselves and possibly making mistakes along the way. This is exactly what a team in MIT is working on. They have been able to work with a machine learning algorithm that can look at scans and then give an analysis in a much faster and more efficient way than the provider can do on their own.

Of course, this process is not meant to replace what the doctor can do, but it is there to help make the doctor more efficient. Rather than spending 15 minutes on 25 patients, these images can be done and analyzed in just a matter of minutes, and the doctor can spend more time with their patients and on other things rather than just trying to take a look at the images all of the time.

In addition to this, it is also the hope that AI can help to improve some of the newer radiology tools that will be released, ones that will be able to help with diagnoses without needing to rely on samples of tissue all of the time. These AI image analyses would be able to be useful in more remote areas, the ones that may not be able to reach as many medical devices or have the same kinds of doctors that those in larger areas would as well.

The most exciting part is that it can make healthcare more available to everyone. Telemedicine, when it is used properly with AI systems, will become more effective because patients--no matter where they are located--will be able to use the camera on their phone to send in pictures of things like cuts, rashes, bruises, and more so they can determine if care is really needed, freeing up the resources of the hospital and saving time for minor things and do not really need to be seen by a doctor.

Surgery Assisted by AI

Another healthcare industry benefit is the use of AI to assist with some kinds of surgery. With a value that is estimated to be somewhere near $40 billion in the healthcare industry, robots can take some of the available data from medical records and use this information to guide the instrument that the surgeon is using at the time. This can help to make the surgery more effective, reduce the amount of time the patient stays in the hospital up to 21%, and so much more.

While this may seem a little bit scary to have a computer work on your surgery, it has quite a few benefits. First, it is not as invasive as some of the other surgery types out there, and this helps to keep the scar smaller and improves the healing time. At the same time, the robot can gather up data on other operations similar in the past, and then will tell the surgeon about any new surgical technique that they could use as well. The results at this time may still be newer, but they are positive and promising.

In one study, 379 orthopedic patients were looked at. It was found that when they underwent an AI-assisted procedure, they had five times fewer complications compared to those who just had the surgeon do the operation on their own. In another study, a robot was chosen to do eye surgery for the first time, and the most advanced surgical robot, the Da Vinci, allows the doctor to go through procedures that are pretty complex with greater control compared to some of the approaches that are used on regularly.

Another example of how these AI-assisted surgery robots can help is in the case of Heartlander, a miniature robot that can help out heart surgeons. This little robot can enter into a smaller incision that the surgeon puts into the chest to perform both mapping and some therapy over the hearts surface. This helps to make heart surgery less invasive, more efficient, and makes the patient heal and get better in no time.

Virtual Nursing Assistants

Ai can also be used in the hospital to work with virtual nursing assistants. From being able to interact positively with the patients who come in to directing the patient on where to go, you will find that these nursing assistants can be effective and could save the healthcare industry at least $29 billion a year, while helping to fill in some of the gaps that show up in this industry.

Since these kinds of nurses are available every day and all day long, this can make things easier for the patient as well. They can be there to answer any questions that come up, monitor how the patient is doing at different times, and even provide some quick answers without having to bring in a person to handle it. These can make them a lot more effective than what their human counterparts can be sometimes and will be helpful especially with hospital and clinic shifts that are short on staff.

Administrative Tasks

This kind of AI comes in use when you are working with the medical field and how the administrative part of this business will be able to interact with their customers. These types of machines would be set up in order to help all of the health care providers there, whether they are nurses, doctors or someone else, save time on getting their tasks done on a day-to-day basis as well, freeing them up to take care of the patients better, and ensuring that everyone gets their job done on time.

Technology, including transcriptions that go from voice to text, could make it easier to order the tests that a patient needs, prescribe the right medications, and even write out the notes for charts for the doctor. When the doctor can get these things done more efficiently, without having to sit down and do them on their own or having to hire someone to follow them around to do it, then it saves a lot of time and money and makes for happier patients.

One example using the AI tools to help support administrative tasks is the known partnership that happened between IBM and the Cleveland Clinic. This Clinic is currently working with IBM's Watson to mine big data and to ensure that physicians can provide treatment experiences to their patients that are more efficient and personalized in the process.

One of the methods that the Watson program can support physicians is that it can take in thousands of medical papers with the help of natural language processing and uses this information to help make treatment plans that are backed by research and are more informed than before.

As you can see, AI technology is can help the medical field out and can ensure that it will be as efficient as possible in many different ways. And we were just able to touch base on a few of the option! There is so much that is already being seen with AI in the medical field, and as more of this is developed, this is likely to become some of the norms as we move into the future.

Chapter 4

Ways AI Affects Marketing and What We View Online

One place where you may be a bit surprised that AI causes a big stir and is already put to work to help out with is the world of marketing. Yes, that is right; many of the big companies out there who are already reaching you in many different ways are also working with AI to help with some of their marketing campaigns. This is because AI makes the marketing more targeted and more effective, helping to make sure that the business is going to make more money in the process.

AI helps out in a lot of different ways with marketing and how a business works to reach their customers. From giving recommendations on which products you should purchase based on your past browsing or purchase behavior or what ads are going to show up on your social media account or on some of the websites that you view, this kind of technology helps marketers do their job so much better. There are many ways that they can use AI in marketing, so let us take some time to explore how these will work.

Providing Content and Good Recommendations

This is one thing that a lot of marketers work with already because it ensures that customers see the recommendations that are best for them, which increases the likelihood that the customer will purchase another item and increase the amount they spend. If you have been on Amazon and looked at some of those recommendation sites, then you are already familiar with how this is going to work for you. We may not have realized that there were some deep learning and artificial intelligence that went behind all of this, but this is done to ensure that the right products show up at the right time for your customers.

Optimized Headlines for SEO

This can commonly be known as clickbait. You want to make sure that the headlines you are providing to your customers can get their attention and are likely to make them click on your page. If the customer never even gets to your page to look around, you are never going to make the sales that you want. But we all know that most of the headlines that are used with clickbait are formulated at best.

The good news for marketers in every industry, especially if you are one of those suffering from writer's block, is that researchers in Norway are learning how to work with neural networks and deep learning in order to write the headlines for you. This can ensure that you get the right headline to attract your customers each time, even if you are struggling to come up with the right one for your needs.

Search Functions

One example is with some of the search functions that show up on the marketer's website. These queries are unique because they can send out a target straight to your website or social media, and once the person is there, they will more likely take a look around and probably make a purchase as well.

You may recognize RankBrain, a machine learning technology example which is popular on Google, because it can analyze both the search queries that are spoken and written, then process these into the search results that will match up with what you want in the process.

Of course, though, it goes a bit further than some of the traditional searches that may be used because it will not just return the keywords and the phrases that are listed out. This is because it is responsible for comparing each of the various queries it receives to some of the others that come in, and then the similar queries return the one that is most likely to fit with what you are looking for. This makes it more personalized and easier to work with in the long term.

Ad Targeting

It is common for a lot of marketers to use the idea of AI to help them to target the ads they provide to their customers. This makes it more likely that the right person will see the information, hopefully at the right time. When you are seeing an ad meant for you and matches up with your wants and interests, you are more likely to click on that ad and check out what is on the other side. And once to the website, you are also more likely to look around and make a purchase. This is exactly what the marketer is trying to do with their targeted ads.

The AI algorithm can be set up to learn from your searching habits and what you liked and enjoyed in the past and then will use this information to send targeted ads to you. This is done over time to help match up with your interests, your searches, and more, in the hopes that the ads will be what you want to look at. Sure, there is a learning curve here, and sometimes you will not see ads that interest you at all. But often, these are successful, and they bring in these big businesses a lot of money in the process.

Even though it may sound a little strange that we are talking about marketing and something like artificial intelligence, many businesses and marketers in our modern world are using the two together to accurately reach their customers and to ensure that they can get the most money for their investment in the process.

Chapter 5

Has Society Accepted AI?

While many of us may not realize that there is so much of the artificial intelligence happening in our lives today, for the most part, it has been accepted pretty readily. Many different types of programs and machines already use this technology--or at least use a subset of artificial intelligence--to help them run, and we use these in our daily lives without even thinking about it.

Sure, when most people hear about artificial intelligence, we assume that this is something far out of reach, something that only those who have worked with the world of technology. But, in honesty, if you have worked on a search engine, seen an advertisement show up on one of the websites you were visiting, or ever used voice recognition software like Alexa, then you already have some experience with this artificial intelligence at work.

We may not think that we will accept AI or that we will ever use this in our own lives, but you likely have, and it will keep growing. This is not a bad thing at all. Accepting AI and using it in other parts of our lives regularly can be good for everyone involved. It can make your life easier, can help us to explore new technologies, can help businesses to be more successful, and can help us to do our jobs so much better than before.

Many of us may not understand or realize when this artificial intelligence is being used in our lives, but it is there, and it is very important. Many tasks are already seen as very common to our lives, and the processes behind these actions will be run by artificial intelligence. Just because we did not realize the technology was there and doing all of the work does not make it any less important. And once we start to see all of the places that this artificial intelligence can show up, you will start to feel more accepting and open to using this kind of system as well.

Let us take a look at some of the simple daily ways that AI is already being accepted in our society, and we may not even realize it. These are not the only examples of how machine learning and artificial intelligence being used, but they are great examples that will help us to see just where this kind of technology is right now and how it affects us directly.

First, have you ever worked with a device that you can talk to? One that you can ask a question or give a command and it responded. This could be on your phone asking a question to do a search or to find directions or on a TV or a device like Alexa. All of these are being run with the help of machine learning, which is a subset of what we will find with artificial intelligence.

The machine learning on here works because it helps the machine to recognize your voice patterns and what you are telling others. There is no way that a programmer could go into things and figure out all of the phrases and requests that you make ahead of time, as well as all of the different word choices, dialects, and even languages. Because of this, we use machine learning so that the program can start to learn as it goes, getting better and better all of the time at figuring out what the user wants.

This is why in the beginning, it often seems like the item has trouble picking out what you say, and there are usually a few bumps in the road. But if you have had the device for some time and has worked with it during this time, it becomes a lot easier. You will be able to make requests and ask questions without any problems along the way.

Another example of this is when you do a search query on your favorite search engine. We have all spent some time looking online to find out information, to look up a phone number that we need, to ask a question, and so much more. And we all likely have some of our favorite search engine that we need to use regularly.

These search engines are also based on the idea of machine learning. It can watch your queries and the results you pick along the way. It will then provide you with suggestions based on that information. The more time that you spend with a particular search engine, the better the results will be when it comes to what you are looking for. And this is because the algorithm behind the search engine is set up to learn your preferences along the way.

You can also see this at work when you go on a website or even on your social media accounts and notice that there are specific advertisements based on some of the websites you have visited before and some of your interests. We have all gone onto a website and seen all of those advertisements on the side and the top of the page. Those are there to help the person who runs the website or the blog make some money, but marketers can target these now to you specifically, making it easier to get you to click on it and make a purchase than it was before.

This is why it seems like the advertisements on your page are more targeted to where you have been in the past and some of your likes. The marketer wants to make a sale for the work they are doing. They do not want you to go to their advertisement if you are a guy and they sell women's dresses. You will unlikely click it, which is a waste of their time and money in the process.

Through machine learning and some of the algorithms that come with that, we find that the ads you see on these websites are more targeted to you and what you like. You may not click on all of them, but when the ads are targeted to you and what you are the most interested in, then it is more likely that you would click and make a purchase, and this is what the advertisers and marketers are hoping for.

If you spend some time on Amazon or other websites that provide you recommendations based on what you were viewing or what you have purchased in the past, then this is a sign of artificial intelligence as well. These companies work with the various algorithms to ensure that they can match up you with other customers who bought similar products or other products that are already similar to what you have purchased or at least what you have already been browsing through.

The hope with this one is that you will see the item, like it, and make another purchase. This is not going to get every customer, but many marketers know that it is a great way to make a bit more on each customer and to get repeat customers, increasing their bottom line. The recommendation system has to take some time to learn the buying habits of the customers and what they like to purchase and more before it can get good at its work. But, over time, it will improve, and the customer will become more likely to make an additional purchase.

These are just examples that you will use daily, but there are many more that you most likely encounter regularly and you do not think about them. Have you ever had a time when your bank put a hold on your card or alerted you because they thought fraud was going on? Whether or not someone else was using your card (sometimes, these make mistakes), there was a fraud detection service in place, run by artificial intelligence, that was there to keep your financial information safe.

Have you ever done an application for a loan? It is likely that a machine set up with artificial intelligence, and not just a loan officer, had a glance at your application to see if it is up to their standards. The loan officer would go through and double-check on things to make sure that it all met the requirements, but the smart machine would be able to glance through them fast ahead of time and saves the loan officer time and work in the process. It is possible that, when you are rejected for a loan, it is due to a machine run by artificial intelligence rather than another human.

Even our airfare can vary when it comes to prices. Some of the bigger airlines will set up an algorithm that will raise the prices on the days that are busier for purchasing tickets and lower on not-so-busy days. This is why we can see such big variations with the price we pay for airline tickets based on when we purchase and where we would like to take a flight to for our trip.

Machine learning and artificial intelligence are newer ideas that we are still learning about, and that we may not know all that much about yet. But this doesn't mean that there isn't a lot of potential that can come with this and that we can use for our own needs. And with all of the neat technologies that come with machine learning and artificial intelligence, we can see that many people in society have already adapted and welcomed this kind of technology. As more time goes on, it is likely that this acceptance is going to continue growing as well.

As you can see, machine learning and artificial intelligence show up in your daily life in so many different ways, even if you did not realize that they were there to start with. This kind of technology is starting to take over and, slowly but surely, it is taking on some different roles that help to make our life that much easier overall. And as time goes on, certainly, this kind of technology is just going to keep growing, and we will start to see more artificial intelligence creep into our lives as well.

Chapter 6

Will AI Really Replace Our Jobs?

One thing that many people worry about with artificial intelligence and all of the different parts that go with it is whether or not this kind of technology is going to take over our jobs and put us all out of work. This is a big concern to a lot of those who do not like the idea of machine learning and who want to be able to stop the progress it is making. In honesty, though, thinking that artificial intelligence--even though it can do some amazing things--can kick us all out of our jobs as our world today is giving this kind of technology too much credit.

A lot of people are worried that in a few more years, most of us are going to be out of a job, and we will have to figure out how to handle the wealth distribution and more that will come with machines taking over our jobs and everything else that we need to handle. What will we do with our time? How will we decide who gets what money and how much? Who is going to be responsible for the machines when they break or for making sure that the machines do the job they were designed to do?

These are all questions that a lot of people have, and as this kind of technology starts to grow and become more prevalent in our daily lives, it makes sense that more people see its power and worry about the future. The good news here is that artificial intelligence is not being designed to take over our world and do everything for us but to make life easier, to improve our efficiency, and to make us better at our jobs. And it is there to help out with some of the employee shortages that are likely to come in the future as our population shifts the kind of work that they do.

This does not mean that we are all going to lose our jobs to artificial intelligence and machines. It simply means that the way we live life, and the kind of jobs we have, may change. And that is something that has happened often throughout history, and we are still seeing that we hold jobs, even if they are different types of jobs than we had in the past. Artificial intelligence is here to help us, to make us better at what we do rather than replacing us and making us go without a job.

We are not all going to lose our jobs; this is not the point of this kind of technology. Instead, it is there to help us to do our jobs better, and to assist us, rather than replace us. It can come in and make doctors more effective at diagnosing and finding problems with patients, but it will not replace the doctor completely.

Works with Us, Not Instead of Us

While many fear that artificial intelligence can swoop in and replace us, and we will end up with no jobs and robots doing all of our work, this is not the reality that we are already seeing with the available artificial intelligence. In fact, instead of seeing this replace the jobs that we have in the job market, and kicking people out of these positions, artificial intelligence is helping to make those who are already in these positions more efficient at what they do.

Many different industries are employing technologies with artificial intelligence, and they are seeing a lot of success. Marketers can use this to figure out the best way to target their customers. Doctors can use this to get through information more quickly and provide better service to their patients. Banks can use this to pick out the right people to give loans to and to make sure that there is not any fraud happening.

These people are not losing their jobs; they are just learning how to do their job more efficiently and effectively. Think back to the marketer. The artificial intelligence is not kicking them out of a job. But it is coming into play and making sure that they are promoting the right advertisements to the right people, helping the business to generate some more income in the process more naturally.

Think back to the example of the doctor. Doctors can use this kind of technology to help perform surgeries, help with patients, and look at some of the imaging that they do. This does not mean that the doctor is getting kicked out and will lose a job in the future, but it does mean that they can provide better results to their patients, and they will be able to do so with more accuracy and speed than possible by themselves. This is definitely beneficial to the doctor while providing a lot of benefits to the patient as well when they receive better care and attention in the process.

When manufacturing decides to add this kind of technology into their warehouses, it doesn't mean that all of those workers are just sitting back and watching them work, or that they are being laid off. But this technology is making sure that the company is as efficient as possible, that he workload is easier for the workers and that the amount of waste that is found in the company is much lower than it would be in other situations.

These are not jobs being replaced in the market. Instead, those who hold onto these jobs find that this is a way to become faster and more efficient at their jobs. And it is saving companies millions of dollars across all the various industries using this technology.

Help to Fill up Some of the Job Shortages in the Future

A lot of industries are worried about how they will fill up some of the jobs they have in the future. It is estimated that many fields, such as the healthcare field, will be short workers in the upcoming decades. There just will not be enough people to come in and take on the jobs that need to be taken, and this can harm the industry.

Let us look at how healthcare acts first. As our population ages, doctors are needed more, especially specialists, nurses, caregivers, and administrative assistants to help out with the elderly and their various needs. But when there is a shortage of people to take these jobs, which is likely to suffer as a result of that? The elderly will not be able to get in to see their doctors, get the caregivers they need or other medical assistance because there just are not enough people to fill the jobs, even if they are higher in pay.

This is where artificial intelligence fits in. The technology that comes with this can help to not replace the jobs but to fill in some of the needed gaps. For example, this technology can come in and work as a customer representative, having the patient answer a few questions and then directing them on where to go and even checking them in. This can help to reduce the amount of needed front desk personnel.

In some cases, these machines can be temporary nurses. They are not going to replace nurses but they can help to monitor patients and cut down on some of the rounds and routine that nurses have to do when they are short on staff. When there is not enough time for nurses to get around as often as they should or there is an emergency that prevents them from checking in when they should, these machines can step in and take vital signs and record notes, letting the nurses know if there is something that needs to be checked right away.

This kind of intelligence can even help doctors be more efficient at their jobs. It can transcribe some of the notes for the doctor so they do not have to write it all out themselves, can analyze some of the images that come through to help speed up the doctor's work, and can be used for a variety of other tasks along the way.

We can already see all of the ways that artificial intelligence can help fill in some of the shortages showing up in the job market, and we only looked at the medical field and none of the other industries that are currently using artificial intelligence. This same thing can be found in a whole bunch of different industries, showing us just how useful this kind of technology becomes very helpful as the job market continues to change into the future.

Open up New Jobs

In reality, artificial intelligence may be able to work with some different types of programs and industries in a way that opens up new jobs. For example, when Alexa and the devices that work with Alexa first came out, there had to be jobs created to make the machines (such as the Echo), as well as customer service representatives to help out for any questions. When a company uses these algorithms to sort through a lot of data, there has to be someone there to create the algorithms, do the training data, and then read the results that come out of it.

These are just a few examples. But artificial intelligence was not created, nor intended, to replace us and kick us out of our jobs. And in many industries, the jobs market for those who can work with this kind of programming and do some of the things that are needed with creating these products. We need workers to make the products, programmers to come up with new ideas, and even those who can interpret the data and the trends that these algorithms provide to us. Our jobs are not going anywhere, but Ai will certainly help us grow our economy and even create more jobs than any other kind of technology has been able to do in the past.

While a lot of people worry about how artificial intelligence affect our future, and it will make it difficult to have a job and even maintain that job in the future, this is not something that needs to be a worry or a concern at all. Artificial intelligence can make us better at our jobs, make us faster and more efficient, but not to take over our jobs at all. We should embrace the future that comes with artificial intelligence because it is here to help us perform our tasks better. AI is also important when it comes to improving our lives and the way we do things in the future.

Chapter 7

How Machine Learning Fits Into the Mix

Machine learning is an important part of artificial intelligence. It can help to do a lot of the different technologies that we are used to seeing in this area of computer science. While a lot of people think that machine learning and artificial intelligence are the same things, they are two very different words.

These two terms are not quite the same, but the perception they are the same can lead us to a little bit of confusion along the way. So, it is sometimes worth it to help you learn a bit more about both of these to learn more about what the two of these things are all about and how they are the same and how they are different.

When you are doing any kind of research that has to do with big data, and even analytics, you will see the term of machine learning and artificial intelligence come up all of the time. These can work together, even though we probably should not be using the terms interchangeably since machine learning is a subset of artificial intelligence.

To keep things simple, let us take a look at the definition of each one to help us out. Artificial intelligence is more of a broad idea. This is the broader concept of machines being able to carry out tasks in a way that we would consider smart rather than the regular computers that we are used to working with.

Machine learning is one of the current applications of artificial intelligence-based around the thought that we should be able to hand over money to give machines access to all of the data that we have, and then we allow them to learn on their own, without the intervention of humans and more.

Long ago, artificial intelligence can be

seen in ancient Greek myths. There are stories of mechanical men who were able to mimic our behavior. They may not have had any of these creatures, but they were already thinking about how to work this out, and how they could do it.

To take this further, some of the earliest computers in Europe were conceived as more logical machines, and by reproducing capabilities such as basic arithmetic and memory, engineers were trying to attempt to create a mechanical brain in these computers at this time.

As this kind of technology, and even more importantly, of our understanding of how our minds work, has changed and grown over time. Our concept of what artificial intelligence is can change as well. Rather than increasingly going with some more complex calculations, work in this field spends some more time mimicking decisions like humans can, making the processes and carrying out tasks to be even more human as time goes on.

Artificial intelligence, a device designed to act intelligently, is often classified into one of two fundamental groups, either general or applied. Applied artificial intelligence is the most common method. These kinds of systems have been designed to intelligently trade stocks and shares or to move a vehicle would be what we see in this category.

You can also work with generalized artificial intelligence. Even though these are less common, it is one of the most exciting advancements that we will see happening today. It is also one of the areas that led us to develop machine learning.

With that in mind, it is time to take a closer look at machine learning and how to see it rise and work for us. Two main breakthroughs lead us to the emergence of machine learning as the vehicle which is driving artificial intelligence development forward with the speed it has taken on right now.

One of these realizations, which was credited in 1959 to Arthur Samuel, that rather than teaching computers everything they need to know about the world and how to carry out certain tasks, the computer or the system can teach themselves how to learn, without a programmer being right there to handle all of the work.

The second is a bit more recent, and it is

the emergence of the Internet. When the Internet was released and became more mainstream, it also came with a huge increase in the amount of digital information being generated, then stored and made available for analysis.

Think about how much information is available on the internet right now. You can easily type in any kind of keyword and a bunch of websites will show up. It is unlikely that you would not be able to find thousands of websites for every kind of topic and search query, and more of these are created daily. All of this information helped to get machine learning up and running as well.

Once these two innovations are in place and ready to use, many engineers realized that rather than them teaching the machines and computers how to do all of the tasks through programming, it would be more efficient and a lot faster for them to code the system to think like a human as much as possible. Then they could plug the machine into the Internet and let it utilize all of the information in the world. And that is how we get a lot of the different types of processes and algorithms that work with machine learning that we know and love today.

What Is Machine Learning?

One thing that we need to learn about before we move on with this process is what machine learning is all about. We have taken a look at how artificial intelligence fits in with machine learning, but we need to take a look at some of the basics that we need to focus on the basics that come with machine learning, and why this is so important.

Machine learning is going to be the process of teaching our system or our computers how to behave and learn on their own. Machine learning is a great process that is going to concern itself with the development of many computer applications that are able to access data, look it over, and learn about that data on its own.

This kind of learning process is going to begin with some data or some observations, such as some instructions, and even direct experiences, to help us find the right patterns that are inside our data. The machine is then able to use these predictions to have a better idea of how to act in the future. The main goal with this process is that it allows our system to learn something in a more automatic manner, without needing a programmer there. Plus, the system is able to learn along the way, making the adjustments that are needed as a situation changes.

When we decide to bring in some machine learning, we will quickly find that this process is going to help us analyze a large amount of data easier than ever before. Think about all of the data that a company is going to gather up over time. They can gather up information on their competition, on the industry, and even on their customers. There is too much data out there, and being able to handle the data is going to be a big advantage to help your business to grow more than ever before.

Machine learning is going to come into play with this data. It can help us to create the algorithms that can sort through this data and give us the insights that we need. There isn't much that we can do with that data, unless we can take a look at that data and see what insights and predictions are inside. This is where machine learning is able to come into play.

There are a lot of different things that you are able to use machine learning for. Any time that you aren't sure how the end result is going to turn up, or you aren't sure what the input of the other person could be, you will find that machine learning can help you get through some of these problems. If you want the computer to be able to go through a long list of options and find patterns, or find the right result, then machine learning is going to work the best for you. Some of the other things that machine learning can help out with include:

1. Voice recognition

2. Facial recognition

3. Search engines. The machine learning program is going to start learning from the answers that the individual provides, or the queries, and will start to give better answers near the top as time goes on.

4. Recommendations after shopping

5. Going through large amounts of data about finances and customers and making accurate predictions about what the company should do to increase profits and happy customers along the way.

Of course, these are just a few examples of when you may want to utilize when it is time to work wit machine learning. Any time that you want to create a program that is able to handle some work on its own, and handle some information and decisions by itself, you will need to work with machine learning as well. Many traditional programs can be done without machine learning, but these do not have the power and the strength that you are looking for.

Before we move on, we also need to take some time to explore the three different types of machine learning that are available. These are going to include supervised, unsupervised, and reinforcement machine learning. Each of these are going to handle some of the complex programming that we need to do with artificial intelligence.

The first type of machine learning that we can look at is known as supervised machine learning. This is the kind of learning where a human who is using the system and training the model will need to provide the input, along with the desired output to the system, and then provide it with some feedback, based on the predictions it tries to make. To make this simple, the programmer needs to show the system a lot of examples, showing them the results ahead of time, so that the system is able to learn as it goes.

After the completion of the training, the algorithm will need to apply what it learned from the data earlier on to make the best predictions. The concept that comes with supervised learning can be seen to be similar to learning under the supervision of a teach to their students. The teacher is going to give a lesson to the students with some examples, and then the student is going to derive the new rules and knowledge rom these examples. They can then take the knowledge and apply it to different situations, even if they don't match up directly to the examples tat the teacher gives.

When we are looking at supervised machine learning, it is also a good thing to know the difference between the classification problems and the regression problems. A regression problem is going to be when the target will be a numeric value of some kind. But the classification is going to be a class or a tag. A regression task can help to determine the average cost of all the homes in a town, while the classification would help to determine what type of flower is in the picture based on the length of their petals.

The second options we can work with is unsupervised learning. With the unsupervised machine learning, the programmer is not going to provide any data to the system. The point here is to get the system to learn on its own, without knowing the input ahead of time. this kind of machine learning is going to be more suitable to use in many types of tasks for processing, which can be more in depth than what we would see with some other options.

This means that the learning algorithms that are unsupervised are going to learn just from examples, without getting any responses to it. The algorithm will strive to find the patterns that come from those examples all on its own, rather than being told the answers.

Many of the recommender types of systems that you encounter, such as when you are purchasing something online, are going to work with the help of an unsupervised learning algorithm. In this kind of case, the algorithm is going to derive what to suggest to you to purchase based on what you went through and purchased before. The algorithm then has to estimate the customers you resemble the most based on your purchases, and then will provide you with some good recommendations from there.

As we mentioned a little bit before, there are more than one type of machine learning that you can work with. Supervised learning is the first one. It is designed for you to show examples to the computer and then you teach it how to respond based on the examples that you showed. There are a lot of programs where this kind of technique is going to work well, but the idea of showing thousands of examples to your computer can seem tedious. Plus, there are many programs where this is not going t work all that well.

This is where we are going to see some of our unsupervised machine learning start to work. We can use it to help us to get the system to learn on its own, without a lot of different examples coming in and telling the program how to behave. There are many times when we work with artificial intelligence where we will use this kind of machine learning algorithm.

And finally, we are going to move on to the machine learning type that is known as reinforcement machine learning. For those who have not worked on this topic that much, this may seem very similar to what we will see with unsupervised learning, but there are some differences that show up.

A big difference that comes with this one is that there is feedback, both positive and negative, depending on the solution that is proposed by the algorithm. It is going to be associated with some of the applications where you would like the algorithm make decisions for us, and then these decisions will be associated back to positive or negative consequences. A good way to think about this kind of learning is the trial and error method, similar to how humans are able to learn new things too.

Errors are fine in this because they are going to become useful in the learning process when they are associated with a penalty such as loss of time, cost, and pain. In the process of reinforced learning, some actions are going to be more likely to succeed while others are less likely to succeed.

Machine learning processes are going to be similar to what we see with predictive modeling and data mining. In both cases, patterns are then going to be adjusted inside the program accordingly. A good example of machine learning is the recommender system. If you purchase an item online, you will then see an ad that is going to be related to that item.

There are some people who see reinforcement learning as the same thing as unsupervised learning because they are so similar, but it is important to understand that they are different. First, the input that is given to these algorithms will need to have some mechanisms for feedback. You can set these up to be either negative or positive based on the algorithm that you decide to write out.

How Machine Learning Fits In

As we discussed a bit before, machine learning allows our systems and machines to learn from various experiences and examples, and the machines can do this without being programmed in the beginning. When a programmer starts to do this kind of work, instead of writing out code, they will feed some data into one of the different available generic algorithms, and then the machine, with the help of that algorithm, builds up the logic based on the data it has been given.

Have you ever spent time shopping online? When you were checking and looking around for a product, did you notice on that website that there were a lot of recommendations for a product similar to what you were looking for? Or did the website have a section like "People who bought this product, also bought this" suggestions? Surely, we have all seen this on many different websites, and this is an excellent example of how machine learning works.

Machine learning enables the machine, or a computer, to make data-driven decisions rather than having the programmer go in and write out enough code to handle every possible outcome for certain tasks. The programs and the algorithms that help them run are designed so that they can learn from their experience and improve over time. The more times the program is used, and the more data they are exposed to, the more accurate the program or the algorithm will become.

We are in a modern world full of not only humans but also lots of machines. As humans, we have been able to evolve and learn from the past, not just our pasts but that of our ancestors. This is how we have progressed and got to where we are now.

But then, we have the other side of things. This era includes machines and robots, and this is just in the beginning stages. The future we will see with these machines and how it could potentially affect all of the different areas of our lives is enormous, and, likely, we cannot even imagine what is going to come out of it in the future.

In the world we live in right now, these

machines or robots have already had some programming done before they ever have a chance to follow the instructions that you set. But what if the machine can learn how to do things on their own and they can work and feel like us, while doing it with more speed and more accuracy than we can do on our own? This is all a possibility with the new era of machines and computers that we may enter in the future.

There is just so much that we could do with machine learning in the future, and it is a fascinating part of artificial intelligence that we can focus on. Being able to understand how this machine learning can influence our lives and some of the things we do will help us to see where this technology has come from and where it is likely to go in the future.

When it comes to machine learning, there are three main types: supervised machine learning, unsupervised machine learning, and reinforcement machine learning. These all have the same goal in mind, but how they work and the kinds of algorithms that come with them are a little bit different.

Supervised machine learning is when the programmer feeds a lot of information and examples into the system, like a teacher working with their students. They will provide a bunch of examples to the student, and then test them on that knowledge to see how well it was retained. When it is retained better, the student gets a better grade on the exam, for example. Then, in the future, when the student sees those examples, they can give the right answers. They can also accurately guess on some of the other examples and inputs they are given based on what they learned earlier.

The programmer has to spend a lot of time giving examples to the system to help it to learn, known as the training phase. Then, once the training phase is done--this can be labor-intensive because you have to show a lot of examples--then, the testing phase happens to see how well the program will be able to retain the information and how accurate it can be. Over time, as it learns from its mistakes and more, the machine, even with supervised learning, will get higher accuracy.

The second kind of machine learning algorithm is unsupervised machine learning.

This one is a bit different because it does not rely on a bunch of examples being fed into the system. This kind of algorithm can learn on its own, making predictions based on the presented information and then getting better based on the feedback it receives from others.

A good example of how this works is with a search engine. There are just too many possible queries that someone could put into the search bar that the algorithm and the programmer will not be able to predict all of them. Each person looks for something a bit different when they do their searching. But with unsupervised learning, the program will be able to still get results and can adjust based on the feedback it is getting.

This is why the first few times that you use the search engine, the results may be further down on the page rather than in the first few results. As you use the search engine more, you will find that most of the time, the results about what you want will show up right at the top of the page. This makes your search more enjoyable, and it is possible because the machine learning algorithm has been able to learn some of the behaviors that you like the best.

Reinforcement machine learning is similar to what we can see with unsupervised learning, and many people think that these are the same thing. In application, they often appear to act similarly to one another, but the key difference here is that with reinforcement learning, the program learns based on trial and error, similar to what most humans learn.

In life, we are told how things work and what is going to happen so we already know ahead of time. But sometimes, the best way to learn is to experiment and do some trial and error to find out what will work and what will not. Besides, we are often more efficient at learning when we can make mistakes and fail because then we learn what works and what does not. This is the same kind of idea when we look at reinforcement learning. The machine tries things out, using educated guesses as well, to help give the right output but learns based on whether it is right or wrong at the same time.

With this in mind, we need to also look at some of the different algorithms and more that can show up when we are working with machine learning. One of the most powerful things that you can do with machine learning includes neural networks. These networks are the biggest key to teaching computers how they should think and how they should understand the world as we do. They also do all of this while retaining the advantages that machines can over humans such as a lack of bias, accuracy, and speed.

A neural network is a system for a computer designed to work by classifying information as the brain in a human can do. It can be taught to recognize images and then classify them in the manner that makes the most sense according to the various elements that they hold onto.

Essentially, the system for the neural network relies on probability. This means that it is based on the data that we can feed into it, and from that data, it makes statements, predictions, and decisions with a good deal of certainty. The addition of the feedback loop enables some type of "learning", which happens when the neural network can sense or is told, whether the decision it made was right or wrong. It can then take this information to modify the approach that it decides to take in the future.

Applications that use machine learning

can read a text and can often work out whether the person who wrote that text is complaining, offering some congratulations, or something else. They can also listen to a piece of music, decide if it is a happy or sad song, and find other musical pieces that will help keep the same mood going. In some cases, the machine learning algorithm is set up in a way help it compose its music, using some of the themes that it already has seen, or based on how likely that music will be appreciated by those who liked the original piece.

These are just a few of the options that you can work with when we see the neural networks. Thanks in no part to some science fiction, the idea of machine learning has also emerged that we can use this technology to have better communication and interactions with digital information and electronic devices as naturally as we would with another person we were talking with.

To this end, one of the other fields of artificial intelligence, that kind of goes along the same lines as machine learning, known as NLP or natural language processing, has become a source of hugely exciting innovation over the past few years. NLP relies a lot on machine learning and some of the algorithms that you can use, which makes it so much more powerful and helpful to work with.

The applications that rely on NLP work to understand the communication styles that are natural for humans, whether it is spoken or written out. The algorithms can communicate back with some of the same kind of language. We can use the ideas of machine learning here to help machines start to understand some of the vast nuances that show up in human language and to help it learn how to respond in a way that is most likely understood by the audience.

When we talk about artificial intelligence and machine learning, we can see that our modern world of technology has a lot to offer with these topics. With its promise of being able to automate some of the mundane tasks, while also offering some creative insight in the process, industries in all kinds of sectors from healthcare, banking, and manufacturing can see the benefits once this kind of technology is in place. Keep in mind that machine learning and artificial intelligence are also something else; they are products being sold on consistently, as well as lucratively for some businesses.

Machine learning in recent time has become seized as a big opportunity by many marketers out there. After artificial intelligence was around for some time, it is now being seen as an old trick. This is unfortunate because there is still a lot of potentials that can come with this, and if we put it away now, we are missing out on so much. There have also been some times when we end up with a few false starts along our road to the revolution of artificial intelligence, and machine learning has come into play here because it is like a shiny new toy that marketers can offer to businesses and more.

While machine learning is a type of artificial intelligence, we can call it something new because we have not heard it before and it has not been touted around for a long period of time either. This provides marketers with a way to sell their technology. To keep artificial intelligence around without it seeming old and outdated just because it has been around for a bit of time

There is so much to love when it comes to artificial intelligence and machine learning, and learning how these work together is so important when it comes to how well we understand these topics, how well the topics work together, and more. The most basic way to consider these two topics though is to remember that machine learning is a subset of artificial intelligence, so often, the things that you do with machine learning gives the machine an artificial intelligence in the process.

Chapter 8

The Ethics, Benefits, and Disadvantages of AI

This chapter will help us get a bit deeper into some of the different parts that ensure we will learn more about artificial intelligence and how it all works. Many different parts come with this kind of technology, but not everyone is on board with it, and there are some disadvantages that we need to discuss as well. Both the benefits and the disadvantages are important to help us determine where artificial intelligence should go in the future and to know whether it is the right option for us to use or not.

In addition to discussing a bit about its benefits and the negatives, we also need to look into some of the ethical questions that come in. Many times, we get excited about all the different things this technology can do for us that we do not think about what could go wrong. Looking into how artificial intelligence can be manipulated or used wrongly and how to make sure that the program does not show any bias from its programmer can determine how we can handle the changing artificial learning algorithms in the future.

As we can already see, many things come into using artificial intelligence, and it is not always as easy to focus on as we may think. This is not necessarily a bad thing, but we must not just jump in and go all in without any thoughts. We will also look at all of the angles in this chapter. So, let us dive in and explore the benefits, the disadvantages, and the ethics that come with artificial intelligence.

The Benefits of Artificial Intelligence

As we have stated throughout this guidebook, working with artificial intelligence comes with a lot of benefits. There are so many different industries that use this technology as well as so many different ways it can be utilized. With that in mind, we have to take a look at some of the various reasons why individuals, especially companies, would want to use this kind of technology to help them out.

These machines reduce error rates. When you use a machine that has artificial intelligence on it, we will see that the risk of error is lower compared to the work that humans do. This is one of the biggest advantages because it can save some industries millions of dollars. With the use the information that is already in artificial intelligence, along with some of the algorithms with it, the decisions for a company can be made quickly. The results are not only fast and easy, but the accuracy can be a lifesaver to a lot of different companies.

Artificial intelligence is also fast and results in some quick actions, much faster than what we see with what a human or even a team of humans can do. Artificial intelligence can make decisions and work quickly. The brain of the machine, which is integrated with artificial intelligence, takes actions so quick that it can help to provide you with results in no time at all.

It also helps out in daily work. Are you already using Google Assistant? Do you work with Alexa and some of the other voice-activated assistants daily? Do you have a Smart Home and you have to speak to it to get things set at the way that you want? If any of these sound familiar to you, then you can already see how artificial intelligence can help you out in your daily work.

Working without brakes is another benefit that you get with AI. As a regular person, we need to take a break after we do so much work. We all get tired; our brains are not designed to work 24/7 all the time without any breaks. We need time away from work, a break, and some time to relax and do what we want and what we enjoy rather than working all of the time.

This is normal for most of us to deal with, but it can slow down work and productivity. When we work with an AI machine, we see that it does not get tired and it can work without all of the breaks. For many businesses, this can be good news. The machines that are integrated with artificial intelligence can work for a much longer duration of time at a high speed and a high amount of accuracy at the same time.

Artificial intelligence machines are better at assisting than humans. These kinds of assistants can make much better decisions without adding in the emotions and biases we see with humans. Sometimes, these emotions and biases are good for us and can help with decisions, but often, they get in the way and they will cause us to make poor decisions along the way. This becomes less of a problem when we work with artificial intelligence.

Since the artificial intelligence machine does not have to work with these emotions, they can work efficiently without having any personal issues in the process. Besides, when we look at how this technology is used as a chat bot, we see that they are designed to chat about the problems that will help a human find their solution, and nothing else, so the emotions are kept to a minimum.

For the most part, these machines can reach much further than we would be able to do on our own. Due to a lot of the risk that comes with it, there are some places, and sometimes some circumstances, where humans cannot reach. Think about something like a fire, an important location for the military, and even some projects that take place out in space.

When these kinds of situations occur, rather than taking on too much risk along the way, a robot--one that has been programmed with artificial intelligence-- would be able to complete the task and it can be done without any human interaction. Such a machine, if it is done and programmed correctly, can do the work and reach places where humans are more limited.

Another benefit is the utility there is for society. We mentioned a bit earlier about the chat bots. These are helpful because they can listen to a voice command, then it will go through and translate it for someone who does not know that particular language but who would still like to talk.

This is just one example of how the artificial intelligence can help out the society. Another one is with the idea of a self-driving car, which you can use to reach the location that you want, with better road safety and no crashes in the process.

And finally, we can look at how the idea of artificial intelligence can benefit us with some of the possible future innovations. Right now, one example of using this kind of technology is with Google AI, which is already looking at how it can be implemented in Biosciences and Healthcare. Recently, you may have heard about how this process will be able to detect things like diabetes by determining the retina depth. And if it is used properly, it can find more common diseases in humans and help us to get more benefits for our health in the process.

The Disadvantages of Artificial Intelligence

While artificial intelligence has a lot of benefits, and it seems like more and more people and businesses are coming on board with this kind of technology and trying to use it for their needs, some disadvantages come with this process as well. It is not always as positive as you may think, and while a lot of companies decide to use it for their needs and to help them grow and provide better customer service for their customers, there are some times when it is not the best decision for you.

What are these disadvantages? And how can you tell whether using artificial intelligence is the right option for you? Below are some of the disadvantages that you can watch out for, and at least consider, when it comes to the growth of artificial intelligence and using AI in your business.

Artificial intelligence can be too expensive. One of the biggest problems and one of the main reasons why people choose to not use this in their business is that constructing a system or a machine that uses this technology can be expensive. Think about how much work needs to be done in this process to make things work and how much it will cost to have enough power, to make the algorithm, to sort through the data, and more. For some big businesses, this cost makes sense and can save them money. But for some of the smaller companies, the cost is just going to be too big and they will forgo using this process.

Because AI-integrated machines are very complex, they cost more to maintain and use. In addition to this, they also cost a lot to keep the system up and running as well as the repair. Artificial intelligence is relatively new right now, which means that these machines, even though they may be relatively new, have to be updated constantly with the changing technology.

Next is that they do not have any emotions. Sometimes, this is a good thing, but other times, it does leave something out that we need as well. Humans are emotional and highly sensitive, which is what makes us human. This is something that we have been able to get from nature and makes us unique and who we are.

Instead of having emotions to help guide it, artificial intelligence relies on coding and programming. Deciding in some circumstances does not work with these programs, and sometimes, it is based on emotions. You will not be able to do this the right way with artificial intelligence, and that can mean that some decisions are not made correctly.

The artificial intelligence machine does not have any continuous self-development. A lot of times, humans learn a lot from the time they are children up until they are adults and so on. This is natural with humans and it means that they can learn and self-develop at the same time from the experiences that they had in the past. But this is not something that we see with artificial intelligence; it does not have any experience really, but will be based on the programming it has been given. The machine only has a chance to "learn" something new if we take the time to update the program.

The AI machine does not have any

innovation by itself. As we take a look at humans, we can see throughout the years that they have always been creative. This is a gift that we have been given by nature, and all of us have different levels of creativity. Some of us are creative with writing, some with drawing, some with music, some with coding, and so on. Each of us has a different type of creativity, but as a whole, humans are born with some kind of creativity, and this is the basis of our developing world right now.

But, think about a machine. Does that machine can do something brand new and be creative on its own without the programmer? Artificial intelligence, at least now, has not been built to handle this kind of process. It can help us in a lot of different ways. It can be useful for businesses and the customers in many cases. But for now, at least, it cannot handle anything like creativity and innovation all on its own.

The last disadvantage would be the idea of human replacement. The machine that uses artificial intelligence can indeed help us out in many ways and sometimes do things that are not within the reach of us as humans. But it can never completely replace what a human can do.

This is beneficial in many ways because it ensures that we can all still have our jobs in the future. But it can have some issues in industries that face shortages with enough employees to help get the work done regularly. While we can take artificial intelligence and get it to do a lot of neat tasks for us and help to pick up the slack, it is not human, and there will be some glaring aspects that show up with this over time.

This is just one of the ways that artificial intelligence can help us benefit society. This technology is just getting started, and we are likely going to see it grow and change more over time. But we need to make sure that we are aware of some of the disadvantages and not just focus on the benefits, or we will miss out on some of the important parts of AI.

The Ethics of Artificial Intelligence

When it comes to working with artificial intelligence, there are also a few ethical considerations that we need to take into account. It is strange to think that working with a machine brings up some ethical concerns, but it is something that we need to be careful about. Machines may not learn the information the way that they should or they may also make mistakes, so it is important to consider some of the ethical points that can come with it.

First, we need to be careful about artificial stupidity, and how we can guard against some of the mistakes that come up with these programs. Intelligence comes from learning, whether it is from a machine or a human. Systems usually have some kind of training phase, and in this phase, they are responsible for learning how to detect the right patterns, and learn how they are supposed to act. Once a system is trained properly, they can enter into the next phase, the testing phase, where it will be hit with some more of the sample data to see how well it will perform.

Of course, our training phase, while it can be pretty complete, cannot go through and cover all of the possible examples for the system. There will be times in the real world when the input is something new, something that the system did not see during the training and the testing phase. These systems can sometimes be fooled in manner that a human would not be fooled.

For example, machine may "see" some things that are not there when it comes to a random dot pattern. If we decide to rely on artificial intelligence all the time to bring us into efficiency, security, and labor, we have to ensure that the machine performs as planned, and it can be hard to catch when these mistakes are happening and how they are going to influence our decisions and how things happen.

Another issue is when it comes to being neutral and fair. Sure, it can add in a lot of speed, and the capabilities it has for processing is much more than what humans can do, but sometimes, it is not seen as neutral or fair.

A good example of this is Google Photos. AI is used to help identify people in the pictures, scenes, and the objects. It can do a great job, but sometimes, it can be wrong such as when the camera issues the mark and on racial sensitivity. Sometimes, when the software used to help law enforcement to predict who will be a future criminal, there is often a bias shown for black people.

We have to always remember that, with things like this, AI systems were created by humans, and these humans tend to be judgmental and biased on occasion. Once again, if it is used correctly or by someone who is trying to reach social progress, artificial intelligence can become a catalyst for some positive change.

Sometimes, security can also be an issue. We may think that using this kind of technology will help us do well in protecting against fraud, doing facial recognition, and more, but these systems can be corrupted as well. It is often a question of how AI can be kept safe and secure from those who want to get on and cause some problems along the way.

The more power we see with technology, the more that this technology can be used for not only good reasons but also for nefarious reasons. This can even include some of the systems that can cause damage if used maliciously. This can cause some issues with cyber security and how safe you are when you do some work online or when you use some of your personal information.

We also have to take some time to look at the idea of singularity and how we are meant to stay in control of some of the complex intelligent systems that become popular when we move into the future. This can bring up the questions of whether the machines can become the fastest, strongest, and most intelligent things out there.

While most people realize that the machines and systems that rely on artificial intelligence are more as tools that we can control, there are some of those who bring up the ethical concerns that this process can someday try to work independently of humans, and it will be hard to control what is going on with the system and stop it from causing problems.

Of course, most of the worries that come with this kind of thing are movies and sci-fi stuff and not really something that we need to worry about when it comes to this process. The machine is meant to do what the code says and will not interact with the world in any way than it is set up to do. If it is set up to work as a search engine, it finds the results to search queries. It will not have emotions or view the world and do things in any other manner than how it relates to that job.

And this is the same no matter what kind of system you are using with artificial intelligence. It can be smart and intelligent, but only where it is designed for. Anything outside of this is not in the capabilities of the machine, so the machine going out of control is kind of silly to think about. If the program is not working well, then it just needs to be turned off and not used any longer.

Another concern is how machines can affect our human interactions and behaviors. Artificial intelligent bots are becoming so much better when it comes to modeling the kind of relationships and conversations that humans have regularly. They will not have the emotions or the same meaning behind them as humans do, but they can model this pretty convincingly along the way.

In 2015, a bot named Eugene Goostman won the Turing Challenge for the first time ever. In this challenge, the human raters would used text input to chat with an entity they did not know, and then they would stop and guess whether they had spent their time chatting with either a machine or a human. Eugene Goostman was able to fool over half of the human raters, and many of them left thinking that they had been talking with a human, rather than with a machine.

This milestone is just the start of an age where we may learn how to interact with machines as to how we react with other humans. This could be seen in our regular lives someday, but often it is seen more in things like sales or customer service. While humans are limited in the amount of kindness and attention they can give on someone else--all of us have our bad days where we are not going to have the best day--artificial bots can step in and channel in virtually unlimited resources to help build up the relationships that they need.

Even though we may not realize it, we are already seeing a time when these machines can trigger the right reward centers in the human brain. Think about video games and clickbait headlines. These headlines are often optimized with the use of

AB testing, which is a beginner type of algorithmic optimization for content that has the main goal of capturing our attention. This, along with some other methods, is used to help make mobile games and videos more addictive.

But, is this necessarily a good thing? It often depends on how technology is used. If it is causing addiction and just lining the pockets of a big corporation and harming the customer in the process, then it is a bad thing. If we can harness the software for something good and use it correctly to help nudge society as a whole towards behavior, that is more beneficial overall, then it can definitely be a good thing.

Many good things can be seen with this kind of technology, but the reason for it being developed and the minds behind it determine whether it is used for good or for something bad. Finding a way to monitor how the algorithms are being used and to make sure that technology is used to help people to progress society and not for something more manipulative.

Another concern that some experts have, in specific, when we start to work more with machine learning, is the reward versus punishment as well as the near future ramifications that come with artificial intelligence. Some of the most intriguing of the research is already happening right now, and we need to be on the lookout for how this will shape our world. The two areas where the near future ramifications can already happen will include with reinforcement learning, which deals with punishment and rewards rather than with labeled data, and GAN, or generative adversarial networks, which allows the algorithms for a computer to create things rather than merely assess by having two nets compete against one another.

We can see the first one with Google DeepMind's Alpha Go Zero, while the second one can be seen by original audio or image generation based on learning about a certain subject, such as a specific type of music or like celebrities to name a few examples.

We can take this to a much larger scale. Artificial intelligence is already set up to have a lot of effects when it comes to environmental issues, climate change, and sustainability. Ideally, and partly with the help of more sophisticated sensors, cities reduce some of their congestion. They will have less pollution and will become more livable in the process.

Once you can predict something like this, it is possible to go through and prescribe certain rules and policies in the process. The sensors that are found on cars, the ones that can send in data about the conditions of traffic on that road and at that time, could later be used to predict some of the potential problems that will come up so that the flow of cars is optimized all on its own. Yes, this process is not really in use yet, and it is not perfect. It is just in the beginning stages, and the algorithms are just starting to learn. But, in the future, the algorithm will have time to take in more data and learn, and it will not be long until this plays a big role.

We have to consider also artificial intelligence and how it affects our human rights and our own privacy. A lot of people have been making a fuss about how artificial intelligence relies on big data which is already impacting privacy in a big way. Two examples of this are the eavesdropping that comes with Alexa from Amazon and the issues with Facebook and its Cambridge Analytica. These are just two of the examples of this kind of technology going wild.

Without the right kind of regulations being put into place and with self-imposed limitations in the process, many critics argue that this kind of thing becomes really common, and we are sure to see this get worse.

Even some in the industry worry about this. According to Tim Cook, Apple's CEO, "Advancing AI by collecting huge personal profiles is laziness, not efficiency. For artificial intelligence to be truly smart, it must respect human values, including privacy. If we get this wrong, the dangers are profound."

Many people agree that, when this kind of technology is used properly, then it can improve and benefit our society. But when no one looks after the technology and making sure that it behaves properly, then this is when problems come in.

Companies and entities that choose to work with artificial intelligence need to be smart about the work they are doing with it. They cannot just allow it to collect a lot of information and use it in any way that it "learns" how to do. This puts a lot of people at risk and it can allow those who control it or those who are able to get access to the information the ability to hold onto things that should be private.

Both of these issues bring up the idea that we need to be careful about how artificial intelligence is being used and how we can program it. It is not always as easy as it seems, and being smart and intelligent about it, rather than lazy, can help to get the full utilization out of the technology.

As we can see, a lot of different sides come up when we talk about artificial intelligence--the good side, the benefits, and some of the many reasons why you would want to start using artificial intelligence in your daily life and to help your business to grow. There are disadvantages, which can explain why not every person or business jumps on board and use this technology all of the time. And then, there are some ethical considerations that we need to pay attention to as well.

Artificial intelligence is taking over many aspects of our world; it is likely to grow more into the future as well. Having a good understanding of how this can work and all of the different parts that come together with this can be so important when it comes to helping us understand what artificial intelligence is, what it is not, and what we can expect as it comes with us into the future.

Chapter 9

The Future of AI and How It Will Shape Our World

One of the best things with artificial intelligence is to think about the shape it will take in the future. We can do a lot with this process now, and we can just imagine all that we can do with it as more technology is developed. We can bring in our creativity as well. The idea that we can train a computer to learn and do tasks all on its own is pretty amazing and the future of artificial intelligence seems to be pretty bright.

We have spent a good deal of time throughout this guidebook talking about the topic of artificial intelligence and some of the options we have for using this type of technology. We looked at some of the industries that you can already find artificial intelligence in and even some of the ways that it can be specifically used. We even looked at its benefits, the negatives, and the ethical considerations. Now, let us take a look at some of the things that could be part of the future of this great technology.

As we have discussed throughout this guidebook, there is already a lot of potential that comes with what we use on a day-to-day basis, and it is amazing to think about what is going to happen as it becomes more well-known and used more than ever. We will see how AI works as it is put to the test. Smart technologies that we use in our homes can be developed and changed along the way, helping us to move this technology and these processes to other parts of our lives, and making it easier to get things done.

Artificial intelligence has a lot of different types of applications that, given enough time, can be used effectively. And if they are used correctly and programmed with the right kind of testing and training data, they will be able to improve the amount of productivity, efficiency, and accuracy that an organization or company can enjoy.

The first topic that we need to look at here though is the idea that some people are still not on board when it comes to artificial intelligence. It is growing in popularity, and we are seeing a growing interest in it over time as well, but there is still a decent-sized group of those who are concerned with what this technology is all about and how we can work with it.

But first, we need to understand that AI is not there to take our jobs and kick us all on the street; it is there to fill in some of the gaps to help us do our jobs better and more efficiently, and it will be there to help us to fill in spaces where there are not enough employees and not enough time to really handle the work that needs to be done.

With this in mind, many businesses and individuals are optimistic that the AI-driven shift in the workplace will result in more jobs being created rather than being lost like the big ear is all about. And as more of these innovative kinds of technologies are developed, AI will have a big impact on the economy, simply because it creates more jobs, jobs that require us to have a skill set to implement some new systems.

In fact, about 80% of the people who responded to an EY survey said that the biggest challenge that would show up when trying to employ a new AI program would be the lack of workforce skills. The workforce would have to take some time to learn how to do these skills and implement the AI system to see the results needed and to make sure that these systems are actually going to work. This could take some time and it could be one of the reasons that a lot of the AI system takes time to grow and be implemented. For this to be improved and for some changes, we need to make sure that we have the right kind of workforce in place.

As we have discussed in this guidebook, full jobs are unlikely to be replaced, but artificial intelligence can help to fix some of the areas where jobs can't be filled, and it can help those in certain positions do their job so much better. It can help make decisions, perform some basic customer service skills, and more, and many industries and businesses can benefit from this.

For example, the idea of automated decision is a big part of artificial intelligence; it can be held responsible for a variety of tasks along the way. This is something used in the financial industry to help when approving a loan and determining if it is a good idea to loan money to one customer over another. This industry also uses automated decision to help with issues like financial crime and corruption.

In addition to helping out the financial world, other organizations can benefit from artificial intelligence, even if it is just from the productivity that this instills into the business. When things can be automated, it saves time and can help to make productivity one of the main supplies of the company.

Due to the fact that some of the jobs that artificial intelligence can impact, we need to stop now and address a few of the potential pitfalls that could come when we use this kind of technology. We discussed this a bit before, but understanding them and knowing what things we need to consider along the way can help us to use the idea of AI properly. Below are some of the things that a business has to consider when they want to work with the AI technology.

1. Businesses have to overcome some of the bias and trust issues associated with AI by achieving an effective and successful implementation that will make it possible for all of the people using the system to benefit in the process.

2. Governments who use this need to ensure that any gains they get from AI can be shared widely, or as much as possible, across the whole of society to prevent social inequality between those affected and those who unaffected by these developments. For example, this could be through increased investment into the training to make it happen.

3. With some of the additional cost savings that happen with implementing the AI systems, employers need to also focus on increasing the number of skills that their current and future employees need to have.

To help us to leverage all the power that we can see with artificial intelligence, we must look at issues that could come at the educational level. We need to have the right kind of training data in place or the data will not show up the way that we want. The training and the testing data need to be accurate and correct the whole time or the results that you get from the algorithm will not be as trustworthy as you had hoped it would be.

With this in mind, we are going to take a look at some of the different ways that we can use artificial intelligence in the future. Some of these technologies are in the works right now, while some are just on the drawing board, but it is believed that with the right algorithms and the right type of AI, we would be able to put them to good use and see this as part of our future soon. Below are some examples of how AI can be used in the future.

Automated Transportation

This is something that we already see a bit, thanks to artificial intelligence. If you have ever heard about the self-driving car, then you know that this could be a part of our future. These cars are not complete yet as they still require a driver in the seat to make sure that things stay as safe as possible. Despite these new developments and that the car cannot drive on its own yet, the idea is new and may need some more work and some more time before it will be widely accepted by most drivers on the road.

The first example of the self-driving car that is the best known right now is Google. This has become such a popular idea right now that even the U.S. Department of Transportation has released some definitions and guidelines on the different levels of automation. The car that Google has released is considered the first level on this chart, and then the definitions that were released can go all the way to full automation.

Handling Dangerous Jobs so Humans No Longer Have To

Think about the process of defusing a bomb. This is highly dangerous, and there is a high probability that the person doing it can get harmed. But if we can send in an AI-integrated robot, it can handle the bomb with more accuracy and more speed. And even if it makes a mistake and does not get the bomb taken care of, then it is a machine, rather than a person, that gets destroyed alone with that bomb.

Think about all of the lives that we can save with this kind of technology by sending robots in to deal with some of the more dangerous tasks rather than a human. It could save thousands of lives by taking over this job and making sure that others are safe at the same time.

This is just one of the ideas that we can look at here, and many other dangerous jobs could take people out and use some of this artificial intelligence. Even if the jobs are not as dangerous as diffusing a bomb, we can still use this technology to help take out some of the danger. We can see this with fields like welding (helping the individual to keep away from the hot temperatures and more toxic substances), and even with jobs that are near bad chemicals, in really bad weather conditions, and of tall heights and buildings.

Climate Change and Issues of the Environment

Solving this problem seems pretty tall, and we may wonder if there is a solution and if something like a machine and artificial intelligence will be enough to handle this kind of process.

The reason that artificial intelligence may be able to handle this is that the algorithms that go with it can get a hold of and store a large amount of data and statistics more than any person and any machine that we have right now all at the same time. With all of this data in one place, AI can find some patterns and trends that we may not see in any other place and can give us the right tools and the right information that we need to be successful with solving this kind of problem.

Better Care for the Elderly

For a lot of reasons, life for the elderly as they reach their golden years and beyond will become more of a struggle. And many of these individuals are going to seek some help outside the home to make sure that they are taken care of and can get the assistance that they need during various parts of their life. Sometimes, this starts with just having someone come and check up on them occasionally. Other times, the care may require a bit more than this. This care may also come from their family members or outside help is hired to help provide this personalized care.

AI is not to this stage yet but it will likely be able to provide at least part of this assistance in the future. According to a professor from Washington State University, Matthew Taylor, Home Robots could start being the tool we need to help out seniors with some of these daily tasks. This can help the individual get someone to check on them and help out but it will not cost as much and can fill in some of the shortages that the healthcare industry is expecting in the future.

For those individuals who are not looking to get someone to help them all of the time but who need a bit of help to stay in their own homes, these kinds of Home Robots are lifesavers. They will use artificial intelligence to get all of this done. The individual will still get the assistance that they need regularly as well as a healthier lifestyle because of it while relying on a machine that is run by artificial intelligence rather than a human person all of the time to do these tasks.

Think of how much this would be able to help out an industry like this one. Healthcare workers are becoming harder to hire, and with the aging population, they will be in more need than ever before. Many of these companies in this industry fall short on their staffing needs, and it is the customers, or the elderly in this case, who suffer. With the help of artificial intelligence, and using these Home Robots, some of that can be solved. Individuals will still receive the care and attention that they need, and often at a lower cost.

These are just a few of the different

things that you can do with artificial intelligence, and, likely, some options that we cannot even think about at this time will become the norm as well in the future. There are so many options, and it seems like our imaginations are our limit. The technology is there; we just need to dream it and think it and come up with an algorithm for it, and we are set to go with inventing another use for artificial intelligence.

While it may be impossible for us to take a look at artificial intelligence and predict the exact future that is going to await us with this kind of technology, it is evident that the interactions that we see with AI are already taking over for us. And as more time goes on, and we figure out more that we can do with this technology, it is just going to show itself as more prevalent in our daily lives.

The interactions that we can do with artificial intelligence, including some of the biggest issues that face our world today, the ability to deal with duties that are dangerous for humans, and helping out with care of individuals and automated transportation, can really change our world, and we are likely to see this happen more and more in the future.

The world of manufacturing takes on a new meaning as more artificial intelligence is added into the mix. This kind of technology helps us to see improvements in how quickly products can be sent out, how business decisions are made, and so much more. Right now, we are already seeing that AI-powered robots are working along with humans. Right now, they are just handling a limited range of tasks, such as stacking an assembly, and there are predictive analysis sensors there to make sure that the equipment is always running smoothly and the way that it should for the business.

This is where the technology is right now for manufacturing, but we are likely going to see this expand and change as time goes on. At some point, while these machines will not take over all of the manufacturing jobs, they will be able to take on more responsibilities and can step in to fill some of the gaps that may come with employee shortages in the process.

How artificial intelligence influences our future is the kind of impact that it will have on our current education system. All of us can agree that education is important, and many parents spend a lot of time and money making sure that their children will receive the best education possible. And we can add in some artificial intelligence to the mix to help educate our children better while assisting teachers in the process.

Artificial intelligence can help digitize some of the textbooks being used in school. Some early-stage virtual tutors can help children learn, both in school and out of school, and can assist human teachers with reaching more students and being effective at their methods. And facial analysis can gauge some of the students' emotions to determine who might be struggling with the material, who is bored, and who is actively learning so that the learning experience can be tailored for the needs of the individual student.

These are just a few of the examples of how education and how we teach our children can change the future and influence the world that we are in. When it is used properly, we can find that it can make it easier for the teachers in our schools to do their job, while ensuring that the students are going to get the attention and education that they need.

We can then move on to how media can

benefit from machine learning and artificial intelligence. Right now, many parts of journalism are trying to harness it and use artificial intelligence, and using it regularly provides them with a lot of benefits as well.

For example, Bloomberg is known for using cyborg technology to help it look through a lot of complex financial reports quickly. The Associated Press employs some of the natural language abilities that we talked about before to help with Automated Insights. This is then used to produce 3,700 earnings report stories each year, almost four times more than what we can do just a few years before without this kind of technology.

With the world of news changing all of the time and reporters and staff needing to try and keep up with more news than ever, it makes sense that this industry benefits from the use of artificial intelligence. This kind of technology even used to come up with headlines for the articles that are SEO-approved, making sure that the titles that go with those articles are more enticing to readers.

A lot of different parts come with customer service and artificial intelligence. Many companies use this to help us to understand more about the customer to handle some of the questions and more.

To start with, Google is already working on an assistant with artificial intelligence that can place calls like a human does to help make appointments anywhere you would like. In addition to the words, you will find that the system can understand some of the nuance and the context found in the written and spoken word.

Beyond these impacts that we have had the time to explore, there are likely countless other ways that AI technology can influence our future, and this fact alone has a lot of professionals, no matter which industry they are in, excited for the future of artificial intelligence and the types of technologies that it can produce.

Conclusion

Thanks for making it through to the end of *Artificial Intelligence: A Modern Approach*. Let's hope it was informative and able to provide you with all of the tools you need to achieve your goals whatever they may be.

The next step is to consider all of the ways that artificial intelligence is already affecting so many different aspects of your life. Many times, we use the technology that comes with artificial intelligence already added in and we don't think about all of the parts that come with it or how it works. Hopefully, in this guidebook, we have been able to explore a bit more about it and how this process can help power a lot of the different technologies and processes that we are using daily.

Inside this guidebook, we took some time to explore what artificial intelligence is all about, how it is meant to work, and some of the different ways that it is already showing up in our day-to-day life. While many people may still hold onto images of robots taking over the world and us losing control over the computer system that we created, this is not really what the whole process of artificial intelligence is supposed to be about.

Yes, the machines can learn, and yes, we can teach them how to do a lot of tasks all on their own, but they are not going to work the same as we as humans do and we don't have to worry about them taking over and doing what they want, without listening to humans. Most of these algorithms and systems are set up to handle one kind of task, and a program that uses artificial intelligence and is set up to handle learning how to play chess, for example, will not be able to also play checkers.

This guidebook went into more depth about all of the different things that you will be able to do with artificial intelligence when you learn how to work with it properly. We looked at how it can be used in many different industries including in finance, marketing, retail, and the medical field. And we took this even further to explore some of the benefits and the disadvantages, and even some of the ethical concerns that come with this technology, and how the process of artificial intelligence is going to change in the future.

Did you like this book?

Tell us with a review on amazon!

Copyright

medical or professional advice. The content within this book has been derived from various sources. Please consult a licensed professional before attempting any techniques outlined in this book.

By reading this document, the reader agrees that under no circumstances is the author responsible for any losses, direct or indirect, that are incurred as a result of the use of the information contained within this document, including, but not limited to, errors, omissions, or inaccuracies.